WHO THAT DIVINES

Laura Moriarty

Who That Divines

Nightboat Books
Brooklyn & Callicoon
New York

ACKNOWLEDGEMENTS

Thank you to the editors of *Aufgabe*, *580 Split*, *The Feralist*, *Hambone*, *Jacket2*, *Try*, and *War and Peace 2* where some of these poems have appeared. Thank you also to the publishers of Hooke Press and Slack Buddha Press for publishing the chapbooks *An Air Force* and *Ladybug Laws*.

ISBN: 978-1-937658-19-9

Cover art wrap: *Death of Cythera*, 2013
by Brett Goodroad. Courtesy of the artist.

Design and typesetting by Margaret Tedesco
Text set in Bauer Bodoni
Cataloging-in-publication data is available
from the Library of Congress

Distributed by University Press of New England
One Court Street
Lebanon, NH 03766
www.upne.com

NIGHTBOAT BOOKS
Brooklyn & Callicoon, New York
www.nightboat.org

"Divinity is what we need to become free, autonomous, sovereign."

Luce Irigaray, *Sexes and Genealogies*,
translated by Gillian C. Gill

PRELIMN

The life-and-death struggle for recognition among gendered subjects is the background of ordinary life. It is so ordinary you forget about it. "Ordinary" relates to "order"—row, series, course, array.

The situation or struggle is also ordinary, frequent, abundant and joyful because it's good to struggle or be incomplete. It's good to organize.

There is also the question of what is true, what is knowledge, what fate or faith?

Fairy tales, for example. What is our pleasure in them and where does it lead us? How do we see what we are shown?

And which wave of feminism is this?

DIVINATION

WHO THAT DIVINES

Devises
As Spicer claimed

"I am a geographer"
A case

For belief
But not in the future

Repeats fate
You say follow the map

But I refuse
Further to follow

What you thought
You saw

Me kissing God
Or giving head

What does that
With the unknown depth

Of social debt
Where each word is a vote

And I self-possessed
And you the damsel in distress

Have to do with the death
Alive in my throat?

Or how not to go
Hunted haunted

Divine undaunted
With you as reader

Knowing everything
How not to go on?

A Tonalist Rules

For the game
When we are unafraid
Narrative coincides with meaning
Flatly in love with
Rhetorical continuity interrupted
Only to be taken back up
Like two things in one
Beauty for example
The present and past enter into
A prosody of unfinished gesture
Against formal predictability
Synopsis is predicament
Irony mitigated by shamelessness
Lack of value for the conspicuous
Turning mentioned earlier
Of fate into history
Unable to be made
Unfashionable as the fact
Of particularity
When prediction becomes
Love of that
Chance

GHOST POEM

The story begins
Waiting for the trick
When after life
Death ends

The night goes on
The sick sea
As much as possible
Comes to me

In the form of
But not alive
In the words from
But not dead

We wed or end
Swallowed by
Sick with
And again

ENACTMENTS/OUTCOMES

for Bruce Conner

From my imaginary world

First of the outcomes
We agree to consider
That it was even possible
When out comes the cat
Someone having left the door
Open though not as open

As what later became known
That he believed the stories he told
The figures were linked and overlapped
As they were in the lines of the master
You erased that day
From my imaginary world

Second outcome

Or explosion in an X factory
Lotus brain artichoke
Map of a shell
Grain of a brain
Bright column
Serpent's tongue
Moth stingray trilobite
Vulva volvox vehement
Come to my rescue!
Stop! Stop!
Leaves like silk
Milk spilt
Not a snake but a tortoise
The universe a door the roof
Of the floor above
Feathers an aquarium
The project
To make love with his sensibility
Or makes sense of his love
The face is the only circle

OUR RAGE

As if poetry had a place
The word hotel
A downward spiral occurs
Our rage takes us away
Clock wasted
Pillow ticking
Your head on it for days
For hours mine
The hotel foreign
The argument a joke
Our rage the same
I won't go without knowing
You say and then you know

STAY WITH ME
after John Lennon

Half of all I say
You know

Equals action
Or ocean

"Calls me"
Not saying

What he
Left leaving

His life
But his wife

Stays with him
In her mind

As you with me
In mine

Six of Doom

with words from William Blake

Or sick moon I find
Whose moth fear we bite
Moan and limp with ease
Our eyes kiss the foam
Our fame the dome or cave

Our oath is boot
Our love not cool
Or is cool
As when April
Means seed
And soil reveals
Harp and cowl
To be eye alone

Not happy but in play
Not birth but day
Not said but soul sold
Out at last saying

O sick moon
I find you

CONSOLATORY GESTURE
with Alli Warren

Reverse embrace
Vows to remember
Also to empty
The poet, [wo]man, word and thought
Caught at the beginning of
Bewilderment lucidly
Loss agent and patient
The rhythm of not
Substituting conflationary
Construction with what
"for world read earth"
For earth birth
Worn inside out
As for study unless
Poetry for language
Actual forgetting
"alone and first in the mind"
Disclosing an order
Wrapped in its own joke
Shuttling between both
Limits tremble or
Pretend what "big" idea
Allows nothing left out
Into accord with one another
Like rapture is left or beings
And to save them

Green

Early mugwort
Come here my love play
Blooms for all its
Claim to discontinuity
Continues to be
Born of spring
The prediction machine
You old reprobate
No escape but in
Turns we take
With each next
Local rhapsodic
Suggest away you say
For what it's worth
Ending naked
Glass of green wine
Face of earth

WORDS & SITUATION
with 32 words from Standard Schaefer

If we balloon the lion
Groan the champagne and
Bathe the heretofore vacuum lung
With discretion only then can we
Concoct the realm coin whose
Chthonic revise will troglodyte
The hullaballoo fuse the bulge
Pluck the iota and grip the gridlock
In the jaws of expediency
Finally to discipline the omnivore
Mink the pose
Repossess pluck

THE EVENT

Angel bait
Careless love
Fate based
Anonymous figure
Influx of
Spit or spirit
Edge of the woods
Commenting
I am not a luminist
But faithful to the event

The Modern Dowser

Of wand or rod
We sing when
Dowsers convene
South-red; southwest-green

Free capillary action
Thin layer coats
We who show
North-violet; northeast-blue

Pellicular advantage as porous
Behavior of water learnt then
Deep sand otherwise choked
Vital fecund victorious

Without faith or face but with
Ring at the end of a string
Clockwise for a hen
Opposite for a cock

A diagnostic weapon
We speak of
The restoration of Pluto
But mean love

The weak motion
In physical memory
Called fading
Between divinatory magnetism and electrical lies

Independence of vision
Muscular events
A question of time or tone
East-green; southeast-yellow

A Valentine, several Germans, a Texan and Michael Palmer
Who gave me *The Modern Dowser*
Whose anniversarial
Foundations of castles and alleys, buried gold

Stomping and counting
Heterodyne interference operations
And numerous errors in the application
West-black; northwest-white

Or this simple rule
Modicum equals win
Pendulum stays
Results obtain when

Waves drawn out
Forecast today's
Ground into water
The same rain

TWENTY LINES
with 20 words from Marc Lecard

From the lurch
We skip
Blowing the undercover
Meltwater whose
Forklift leaves
Roadkill scabrous
On the mouldy coast
Yapping
Transfixed
And oozy

Whose vanish
Is tricky
And leafblower
A tool
Or perfidy
As we also say
Knows the deal
The fake
Is ghost
The beast real

TIME TRAVEL
with 22 words from Norma Cole

Stands rash
History his hat
Circus his hammer
Makes camp

Tar drying to
Express the gradual
Commission broke
His skin

His fugue
Being over
The accused swore
At least twice

Ended dark
Suspended sharp
Time enough
Yet not

Non Tonal

after Arnold Schoenberg

Dreams a rule with
Words not mine
Not a body not belief
His lines
Melancholic dusty waltzes
Knowledge of techniques
Technique of knowledge
Imagination overcome
Beautiful nightmare
Opposed to genius
Letters not addressed suggest
New sound or new personality
Deathsick moon
While remaining virtually unperformed
Arousing resistance
Every innovation destroys
What it produces
The bonds of a by-gone aesthetic
Floated into the non tonal
Speech becomes music
With no other aim than comprehensibility
Blacks the sun
Textures rent by incompatible elements
Speech *versus* music
"I feel the air from another planet"
Not a technique but a passing phase
Uncataloged dissonance
Pierrot lunaire
Growing up with the same influences
Emotional revolution
Or a different place and time with the same mind
Having abandoned tonality
We create language not style
With an almost somnambulist sense

Bravely to plunge
"Free" composition and sublime banality
The green horizon
Makes the past accessible to the new feeling
Laughs, spits, hisses, makes animal cries
Maid of the sky
Complains if you do this you are not "free"
To do that
A new geological formation
Serial universe
Obvious musicality
Or universes
Remix ensemble
Not a single thing
Or will be

A Simple

Concoction
Or name
Of one
Unprepared

Green first
Later dark
Dead yet
Flowering

More to possess
Instead of less
More thought
More life

A head
Alive with
A dose or
Cordial

Suspended when
The solution is the problem
Compressed weathered
Worried dried

Cut tried
Not in that order
The same line
Is more

Fragrant
Moxified as in
Burned and
Forgotten

Some wild
Thing grew

For you
In me
Then

Because the substance at the center of our ritual doesn't work we have to plan
carefully. The morning is gray. The horizon blue. Do you see images when
you read? Painters when you look? Musicians when you listen? *Popol Vuh*
appears. Is appropriation appropriate? you ask. Come over here, you say.
Bring the book. Thinking along with the song, you nod. I go back and forth.
We belong to the same inner club. More addicted than faithful. Often stunned
or stained by the sap of the experimental monster we call Our Love. Part
plant, part man, not unlike *The Thing* but he is Our Thing. Our Love
is malevolent and strong. We are someone else to him. Even dogs. He kills the
dogs, then is a dog. He is everyone. He is you. Me.

Laughing he
Can see
Sounds like rain
Extends
Over everything
We know this
Has to look
Changes the book

We text the world. Dawn comes up. There are mountains. We are not
different from them. There is blood and sap. We hear birds and plants. What
is going on? we say, not giving up. Things are familiar. Concocted. Tonic.
We find defeat. We find transformation. We try again. We synthesize. Simple.
Meaning. Time. The solution or amalgam. One ingredient. Soak and dissolve.

Felon Herb
Old Uncle Henry
Potion notion

I know him
All afternoon
Wormwood
Winter

Chernobyl or
Place where
Mugwort grows
Disturbed

Root cup
Clove nut
Or mug
Thwart

In the same valley
And only in this
Valley or saint

John's plant or plate
Goose as in Mother
Or hedge rider

Part poison
Part
Flown
Unless you have

A cauldron
Called a head
Still being
Known

Dermal
Absorption
Simple
Or in spring said

What you do
I know

MUSEUM OF CRIME

1.

Wake into fiction
Talk to self in sign
Disagree disappear
Follow the missives
Evident everywhere
Available nowhere
Is this a clue?
Is there a way back
To your block?
Are you the one who
Says reading is being?
In this book
They say they see
But what do you say?
Don't start don't stay
Don't try or die
Not my song
Or my problem
Something in a box
Something else lost
Are the melodies
And memories removed
From this vessel
Yours?
Am I?

2.

Coming in from out
Deadly as
Measurable levels
When the scale fails
To know how much
Fun with what
How long or why not
Other questions posed

When the gun shows
What can be done
With the moment
But what can't be done?
When out is in
I am real
Gone when I arrive
Alive where no one
Knows to lie
About knowing me
Flutter and sputtering
You out there
What do you want?
When do you go?

3.

Away but
Where away?
Creation Day
In our state means
To be created while
The present sinks
Beneath our feet
Causing us to be
Afloat with or on
The sea of
Lost to
The bay
What there was before
Who knows
Not to say

A Franc Sonic

for Jerry Estrin

Snow covers
The hills one by one
Our neighborhood
Characters become
San Francisco 1874
Words later language
A photograph
At home when
Light writes 1974
Or 1979
We move where
The Lives of My Books
Pages accumulate
Not legible as themselves
Historical time 1989
Startled leaves us
Unafraid though
Overgrown
Died in 1993
Moved in 1994
In pink stone
Earlier in "The Park"
Wrote shells and cherubs
The cathedral
The fountain

QUIET MOURNING

for Leslie Scalapino

A bowl of gardenias
By the Kwan Yin
Though magnolia was her flower
But here on my steps or
There in her house where
In ordinary life
Last but once
I saw her alive
We had tea and sweets
Stuffed with bean paste
Years gone by
Following pleasure
Wherever it worked
We had tea again
And she by then
Only angel food
And determination
Would live still
But wildly
If she could

Unknown Sun

"light which is not sum" —Norma Cole, *Mars*

The workaround or aura
Not like repetition

When we get to the final sun
The maps are water the water gold

He would not honor me
You explain then against

The disbelief displayed by the character
I couldn't know him

But knew love and
Know it through knowledge

"Love never falls off whether prophecies
will be abolished whether tongues stopped"

Announced as the fact
Redolent of what was

The defining addition
More than the parts

Unprecedented
Ardor also not

Adding up to
Sun or son to sum

The outcome
Unknowable

Perfect and
Unavowed

The same sound
Unknown sum

CLOTHO AND THE GOLDEN REMOTE

A Western landscape in the last century. Back then
We played cards like men
A man finds a woman
"by a clue of thredde" (Alfred, Lord Tennyson)
"as if all / the spicery of / The world had been" (again)
Or you could see the thread in another way
The element of chance
In summer snow but it's spring or no
Winter rapidly clouding over and then bright
The ally appears in her guise as a guy
Saying I want you now without care to be
"Out of the golden remote wild west where the sea without shore is,"
(Algernon Charles Swinburne) or Clotho spins
We live in our heads in the West
Which brings us to California where I (you)
Say aloud what I thought
It feels like fear but is fair as far as it goes
"the twirl of the needle stabbing / my spindle
the thread of contention" (Robert Duncan)
The cards can't possibly know
As if all the spicery of the world had been
There then

Notes on Divination

"when I came to my castle" Crusoe says
"The indefinite overcomes certainty" *Dao de jing*, Flood Editions

I Ching
Dao de jing
"Impelled by the dual forces of academic opportunity and war"
The Baroque Encyclopedia of Athanasium Kirchner
Delta Primer
R. Crusoe (versions)
Robinson in Space
various herbals
Robinson method in *Crosscut Universe*
Prospero's Books & *The Falls*
Malakov   Malakoff

Artemedia vulgaris (mugwort)

but how could I know from my place on the road?

"Protected by emanating a dark aura…" *Semina*

The rocketeers, racketeers, spaceports, Martian moon, Phobos, powerful
solar storms, bright orange star, near the infinite Jovian moons

"Am I happy?" he asks her

He said everything old is new again
But the life he imagined

Yesterday dramatic
Today okay

Full knowledge
Shocking passivity

Later the line or
Map in the sand or of sand

The footprint figures except
In Coetzee's *Foe* where the tongue

Becomes the body part we
Notice its absence meaning

A limit like that of an island
Or the planet or the plan

If a rug is a garden
Is a garden an island?

An unnamed ship named *Ariel* in Bunuel's 1952 version
which begins with a shot of the book

"It was most striking to be surrounded by new birds, new reptiles, new shells,
new plants and yet by innumerable trifling details of structure, and even by
the tones of voice and plumage of the birds, to have the temperate plains of ...
Patagonia, or the hot dry deserts of northern Chile, vividly brought before
my eyes."

Charles Darwin, *Journal of the Voyage of the Beagle*

The connection of pirates to Robinson
Of yellow to the time of day it is late
For example or very early in 1965
February 4th and Robert Duncan is awake
Writing and I am 100 miles away asleep & 13
He is 46. My fate is to live where
he lived later and to be here

All times at the same time
I, Robinson, cower in fear

Waltz of Memory & Doubt

In my politicized diary
Waltz occupies doubt
Memory is bright
The ladies come alive
The gentlemen arrive.
We converge on the concourse.
The gentlemen cry
When I speak you speak
Waltz enacts political paradox.
Jerk. Foxtrot. The swim.
How do you do that?
How does your waltz win?
1970. *2001*
The movie not the year
The first drum circle
High school is tense.
College is over
The revolution has begun
Modern man leaves the moon
Only to be drafted.
The historical record weeps.
What do you believe?
What do you do?
Will you vote with your feet?
Waltz abides.
Waltz landscapes the crime.
The banner bares waltz like a virgin.
It's 1968. It's 1969.
There's a war on.
Waltz is bored.
Waltz is three-four time.
Waltz cheats the critical link with a coarse anomaly.
When will waltz stumble?
Why is waltz the crime?
Reflection reaches the citizen
Voting for the first time.

Will waltz capture the ballot?
Waltz scripts its own lines.
It's 1989.
The East dazzles waltz.
The West wants what it wants.

Capitalism is not sublime.
Waltz quibbles over the wall.
Communism falters.
Debt is not a crime
In my day
Waltz hummed libraries.
Curriculum supported waltz.
Waltz dreamt.
Soldiers cried with the gentlemen
The ladies were the women
Or were the gentlemen.
That was then.
The war went on & on.
Then again
The diary speaks
When waltz dreams.
Waltz tweaks city hall.
A demon stretches it out.
Three-four time after time
When we dance
The paperback predicts perdition.
Revolution engages
Can a romance do that?
Motto calculates need.
Fortune costs a fortune.
Waltz fears doubt.
Time alters waltz.
Waltz alters time.
It's 1999. It's 2011.
The synaptic moment explodes.
There's a war in heaven.
Waltz reiterates its call.

Doubts & sings.
Read & believes.
Waltzes around the target.
The war is automatic now.
Autonomy autonomizes.
The gentlemen cry out.
We are not gentle.
The women celebrate
The reflected individual
Remembers to vote.
2012 portends well
Or does it?
The predilection remains.
Not losing is not winning.
Despite everything there is to know about fate.
The war is never over.
Waltz is not a game.

TRANSPOSITION

Not the question of who
Is legible to whom or who
Counts or the diagram
Of that sentence commuted
But what is (trans) sent
Are they real he asked
Real expensive she said
But it was an episode
Not the real poetry
Addresses
The list of which gets
What does it get again?
Is there a transposition
When sound imitates music?
As Duncan wrote
He loved Levertov
In the letters
That make love
Evolve as a consequence
Of telling
What is human swells
What burns red What is
Sound remains strong
Or lists
As when the list
Addresses changes of
Who is read and what is known
That she was a witch
Or just another poet
Eligible for scorn
A sentiment transposed into
Resentment in the best sense
As resent means
Send again to see

Direction as reckoning
Grammar to glamour
Red to end spectrum to
Speculative poetics to a subset
Of text and hex
Violet to violent
"Even as we are most 'sent'"
Letters to love (hers)
Unknown to renown finally
Revealed to (be) each other

Palm Sunday's

Bread of the presence or
A sword appears meaning
War or at least danger
Yields nothing and
Falls away as we
Stumble among weeds
Growing together
As ourselves
Having eaten it
The bread and being present
But hidden in a narrative
Demonstrates
The field is the world
Unbelief and distrust and
Things misbegotten
All of it existed and occurred
The crowd was there
Represented by Salome
Asked for and got the head
Without doubt and strong
Winds out on the sea
Came as an offering
Or human precept
Walking on water
This is later
Merely saying
Listen and understand
How do you not
Get it?
But don't tell anyone
Who doesn't set his mind on
The divine thing
Called transfiguration
Or substantiation
As in God talking away
The day and God's wife

Corroborating His story
Or girlfriend rather
Saying about no sin
And I don't so you might
Not want to judge me
Before judgment comes
The unknown night, time
In the garden, time
On the hill of skulls
Time to remember the debris
Of a life with the rust and dust
We never got rid of because
That part of the story wasn't true
And everything at once is one
Way of looking at what happens
And is also the other way
Breaking down into
Constitutive elements
Like it's almost May and the camellias
Are out and the old cherry tree
By the driveway
Is not quite dead
After all

The Hand Was the First Map

Hand-colored hard won
The map of mistakes
Mass-produced in
Venerable splendor
Took shape
In the wakes of ships
Tracks or paths of explorers
And animals as the apprehension
Of a trail in the mind of a doe
Or boundary line in a bird brain
Becomes a flat surface
A coherent graphic of relationships
Between places in the world we know
A reliable time-keeper
According to hearsay
A map of words
A distorted grid
Engorged to the size of a world
Of hazards and errors
Including lines from
The Last Days of Time
Or the idea of "climate"
Reduced to itinerary
Speaking with and into
The moment of knowledge or
The Collection of Memorable Things
Supplemented by a list of distances
A route to be a map must be
Flattened with practical accuracy
A radical cartographer claims
The map is a game
A place to dwell or denial of same
Each a replica of its prototype
An act of power
Source of doubt
Certainty delight
Place or sense of place
Wall map attached to a wall
Can't get there from here
Can't not

WELCOME DEAR CHAOS

with 27 words from Bruce Conner

Vexed from the start the zephyr
Question unlocked the highly
Polished box unleashing a torrent
Down which anyone would hesitate
To drop though drop we did
Elbow by toe by fist by thumb
Ending up hum down hanging by
A shoestring kissed by flame leaf
By gold crushed into the applesauce
Inevitable once the butterfly
Wing released the chaos theory we lived
Or died by nothing was left but to
Bark at the dream or begin again

Thumb to fist as if only when we start does
The question of the flame torrent
Down the fist of its bark becomes known
To us though to hum was enough to
Make applesauce into gold and let
The butterfly escape the thumb of
The chaosophist, the leaf to wing
Into the dream to polish the zephyr
Until nothing is left but a drop
Or a shoestring and to elbow
Or toe remains the only way out

There were more wings and more cards. The leaves in the cream were
iridescent. They were inevitable and venerable like Holmes himself. Moriarty
was missing. Everyone was suspicious and resistant. No one could keep
track of the results. The address was clear. It was like me to you only not.
The phrase "fellow visionaries" was an accusation. You were the accused,
the accursed.

Zephyr she screamed but too late
He like a leaf elbow over toe had
To wing along drop by drop
A shoestring away from flame
He put his fist down the thumb of the

Butterfly answering the question
Of how to begin hum or dream as gold
As possible while not forgetting to polish
The torrent with the applesauce of desire

But there was no polish to the dream of lists
Other than what was toe up or fist down
She was like a butterfly to me or other bug
Wing, hum, flame she had it all
I can't speak about the applesauce but of
The zephyr I can go on in torrents
The question was the start the focus
The other side of the card where the shoestring
Was arranged by thumb to invoke the bark
Of drop drop drop where the elbow is the
Throat of the leaf set to begin on time

Applesauce was nothing to me then
Chaos thumbs the hum off the zephyr
The unspoken torrent becomes the question
The leaf gold the butterfly flame the drop dream until
Finally the applesauce and so on

Overwhelmed with clues, Holmes comes home. Words dance in his head
like men. Everything is evidence of something. Counterintuitively, the
problem on the game board does not repeat. There is in memory the
expectation of the symmetricality of events, but there is nothing on either
side of the cards that would allow us to believe in such a result. The
impossible becomes the only alternative when the possible is eliminated.
The game is afoot (toe or thumb) but this zephyr is an ill wind if there
ever was one. It's raining again in the wordland.

LADYBUG LAWS

Ladybug Song

Gone down
And along with

The community and
Path of

Stenciled bugs of the lady
Persuasion (she who) dancing

Down it carefully wild
Patterns for example

Dots and do I have to say it?
Stars surrounded by newly

Minted planets, plants and
What have you for me today?

Lady as endearing meant
To me or means enduring

The astrology of this estrangement
Strong because small

Or not small but young
Or rather derangement

Going off like an alarm
Coming like the summer in

Yesterday was today then
Do don't

Bug me she says
She goes on

Read red as read
Lady as later

Song as wrong

GREEN LADY

with words from Elizabeth Robinson

Civil disobedient whose soul
Not kept or kempt
Not thorough though to her
Thoreau was a game

Faucet or fountain
Mastermind a hunter
Verb cloudy over
Thy crick otherwise known as

Sprain a kid
Bug alias
Mailbox a sigh
Or dark sequel preferably over

Begins again to chasten the stain
Coating the drain down which
She appears to chain the allow
Abet knuckle under

Faucet flounder
Mastermind or underestimate
Thoreau's cloudy head
Also known as The Rover

Who will sigh for the sequel or
Number sprain whose dark
Drain is remiss
Ladybug a game

Mailbox a knuckle
Or tardy bother
Known to abet and allow
They crick to chasten or finally harbor

Coating Thoreau
With herself preferably
A verb now
Faucet off

Chain over
Her soul to keep
Swaps thy for thou
Thee for me

Ladybug Honey

with words from Alan Halsey

Battles and scattering
Calibrated
To assess the meant

Switch to
Its airwaves until
Raining down obtains
The elongation of our nights

Known as a storm
Already not right

Time was Orion
Trumped Iota
But now ladies

More like notes than days
Scribbled into the cyclic
Explode the odd years
Open the even

Horizon sky spot story
Or series of spots
As those here arrayed
Wet with

LADYBUG LAY
after Mina Loy

"Double is as double does"
Doubled down on the divan
Whose divine ones
World arose

"Smaller than my soul"

Emblem album or
Antimacassar being not
After the disaster but
Doily tablecloth or shroud

Whose cut roses evoke
Dead things threaded
A map of circles

Armed or winged
A flyboy sings
The oil of whom
Profitless

Heads against sense
Beauty displayed
Spots alight
Like Martian ice

Evaporates
Dice thrown
Lady naked
Bird flown

Ladybug Story

1.

He loves her because she is well-read. She loves him because he is, well, written. She because he is vulnerable and intelligent. He because she is sure. She is statuesque and spotted. He is shorn. They know things together. They are torn.

She because green. He because red.

He gives into her wit-and-raggedy thing. She to his resistance.

He reads what she writes on herself. She what remains when he has gone, again, down in flames.

He runs then, glances over his shoulder, says, "Nothing! Nothing!"

She keeps busy while she waits. When he returns, she has forgotten everything.

He pretends to be unaware of what is going on. She also pretends. They play this game together awhile, in their heads. Then in the world, they play it again.

The person she knows is more vulnerable than the one he wants to be.

Her own vulnerability is so great he is tricked into believing she is the strong one.

"We are like planets," she says, knowing she is more like a creature in a fairy tale.

"Lady of the Lake, I hate you," he almost admits. "I love you not," he goes on.

He stretches out in lithe candor. "Not a chance," he says.

"Not in deed, or in love, overcome," she responds softly.

"No, not," he says, but stops, lost in thought.

It is their last chance but one.

2.

Now we enter the sweet future as seen by one who, having stopped, glances back. He walks straight into something.

"Fly away," he says, announcing his fate.

What actually occurs involves parallel universes taking the form of a series of lines.

He doesn't know that he is telling the truth whenever he makes a sound.

"When will he wake up?" she wonders, though she knows she is the dreamy one.

"When will she fall asleep?" he thinks back.

They lapse into the present, languishing there (here). They are ready. Or will be.

Tense.

When reality hits.

Ladybug's Lament

with more words from Alan Halsey

Or acrobats cadenza
A cataract away
From disaster
Their movement
A shard and shamble
Their minds
A carp splatter
Able to gyrate
In marmalade only
Dapple in lava

Not I tell you
Mellow the broth
Not gossamer
My heart quails
My salamander
Fuzzy and idyll
By which not
To dream I mean
But whisk or ratchet
Back to acrobats
Who sadly husk
Unable to bubble
They squander languish
And tribulate together

While I drone out
Both sides of my carapace
A tonal iota

Ladybug's Laws

We can barely see what's out there
Overwhelmed as we are by repetition
Though I depend on it for what sense
Of continuity remains to me when
I see you I know I am at work

A rendition of two figures called wings or
Radio Amor but what do we know of that?

A study in red, yellow and black called
The bee stings the martyr
But how can we hear ourselves above the war?
A ladybug is painted on the path
Some writers to their readers are as spiders
But you to me as reader are insectivore
Or creature from paradise

Made of iron with objects attached
To the ground or from the air
Head down Hanged Man (or woman)
Card of suspense or love

My skin is made of your decision
We write with paint on old newsprint
There are poets in the debris by the door
What comes in goes out
Hello name we say
What do you want?

Ladybug

A mental journey with the same hat
The coat more symbolic than practical
The map she made of her head
Looking at me again
The hat like a halo and she

Gives herself like a saint away
To the atelier of another master
Whose walled courtyard, signature blue
And previously unpublished lives
Of the poets influenced you
As when two people
Are the same person

Sun worship we read on the sign
And today is Sunday
This happens all the time
In my life ruled by divination
She sings for me and I see
The line between us
Is the one between things

No experience but in emotion she sings
Cows, crows, bugs, buds
I wanted to read what you had written
But didn't know you then

We gather herbs in our heads
The leaves curled and spiked
From which the ladybug whose
Spots and whose red spread

Of wings nervous because the leaves
In flames and the cup also red
At the portal of the demiurge
Invoked by all this rushing around

The eyes in our names are the same
We say I work or I decide
Spot for spot we go out
You go out

Ladybug

O the cows and crows!
Did it hurt when you got that?
Each spoke clearly visible
The wheel of fortune
An elaborate musculature
Closes around her heart
Or is that my mouth?

Vulgar is another way to say
Artemis left her alone for me
But I don't say it

POE'S BUG

Southern sodden sudden
Coleoptera whose death's head
Read with black or black with
Wings sheathed
Shell or coccinella
Two spotted throb
Gutted twice stabbed
It's rough out there
Larvae larger
Gilded dark
Cloak of sorrows
Lady Luck
Also called love
The Gold Bug
By Edgar Poe
Whose red black
white and yellow
Tarantella begins
With the end
There is nothing left to know
Incidental to the treasure
Not found in the code
A man for a god
Named claimed
Ghoul for gold

FLOWN

Ladybug obvious
Hybrid of bug and lady
Unthinkable state

Diagram, game,
Bug sound
Or anatomy

Laid out but
Would that spot
Count as a gun?

Or are they random?
Lonely bird
Lying lady

Bug me not
You say but
Who am I to fly?

I can't see
What I can't say
I didn't mean gun

But gone
Always already off
Somewhere not

Pronotum or crown
My pronoun for
Your heart

Also not around
But flown
Only the idea counts

Not of but was
Jeff Goldblum
Sloughs off

His human in
The Fly
Animatronically

By definition
Nothing lost when
You take off

One animated anatomy
Away from
Oblivious to

ANGRY LADYBUG

Stunned when lost
Admits which
Spot we're in
As winged when
Nobody fucks with me
Ethic questioned as this
Discipline applied heavy
Handed and in retrospect
Anger beautiful love clear
Bug gone

Imitosis

after Andrew Bird

When what happened
Broached by me and
By you acquiesced to

Someone in sequins
In this sequence
Pinned

Puppet beast of puppet burden
Animate mannequin
Leaves

Read as the green
Of the creatures
Between us

Bite
Spin bet
And win

Without trying
Against
Sense or otherwise

Flagrant
Means
To be real

Available
But never
Together

Again
Or doesn't mean

SMITTEN

What is it with these bugs?

To be moved by figurines or just a job as with me and the Bee?

I produce enormous events.

I can't talk about it.

Later another and then

a bug bounces off my forehead like Japanese beetles when I was a child.
Meant to eat the mosquitoes but were everywhere, replacing clouds of
DDT (another solution) from a truck driving around like the ice cream
man but with no bells. Run after him. Hurray!

Alan Halsey searches for the Ladybug Flu I mention in an email but
finds only

Another outrage of the bug/person barrier

A trick or tick. Not unlike yourself. Be prepared.

Death's head, Buddha's hand, played thing

Better off unread than dead

A Tonalist toys with her ring considering

A spate, spot, pride or pod of ladybugs but written

You move toward me once innocent now guilty

Unaffiliated

SAYINGS

Bitten
Too cute by half
Alone in the dark
Up the creek where
Shit stakes its claim
Save me save me
You as you or
I a lady who
Cries sings
And says wait
Late ones wake
The early dream
Never born
As if selfsameness
A failed technique
Solved anything
But what then
Moves us
Hear me out
Loud with
Bells on
Or better
Married
Carried we

make a connection to that (this) time while retaining a way back. An
argument never ends. You are never right if I am never wrong. Logic won't
help us here. Imitation is involved and reproduction. Assimilation but
not of each other. We sit across a table or in a corner or on a row of stools
against a bar. In a nest or net. We smoke. Everything is possible now. It's
a short story. Events are speeded up. Outside of consciousness we remain.
Outside the frame. We complain, resolve and soon the past is behind us,
the future a trap but not quite. Another story not about nothing. The red
and the black. Ambition. Disappointment. Not meeting or meeting but not
knowing. Or knowing but going. Bug love. But what did we know?

Ladybug Bites

No way to treat
Let's call the gentleman
Whose latest move reveals
Who you are to me to you

Now that you've had it (them)
A way to say lady
If that's what you call yourself
But you never call

More than once
And if luck is also one
How many are there?
Lady an endearment then

Before the birth of one
Much as oneself or
Other such would
Treat like she wants to

Not to be to me
Endearment epithet
Never like she should

Ladybug Bites

May damsel horse dragon
Flat though exact
Whose intended usage
Untraced Neolithic fauna
Baffles the salamander

The fly lowers herself
Where green might gather
Amphibian skulls appear
Bookworms fade

Light grows again
Night mummified
Scattered among icy
Touch-me-not

Flown now or
Fooled by perception
Into being false
She to bleed
He to sleep and read

The music of the animals
Primitive mosses whose surviving
Circles of chalk
Draw us out

I, Ladybug

Citizen
Of the imaginary world
Disreputable
Indisposed
Sorely used
Inordinate
Lay down my rules
And you, ladybug
What do you do?

DESTINATION

PSYCHOGEOGRAPHY

The place protects its own
Giving into you only
If you find and give into it
In turn and unfold the map
Of the trail to the past
Beyond which you wish to go
Or have gone though
You can't as you know
Go when
The feeling comes
Up from the ground
Yet again and
You give in
While the idea of place
Replaces your face
With its earthy smile

Time

Alibi is elsewhere
The unlikely past was inevitable.
The unyielding present precipitates delay or
Infinite decision known as the accusative feminine parsing
The moves through which
Didactic interludes arrest time

The physical world does not have an independent reality but exists as a
perception of the finite mind of others.
Where location equals destination your subject observes
The rules which require the exchange of pieces
To reveal by action motive is no more real than any other revelation.
Pre-existing temporal displacements typically obtrude from the case.
Overlapping events or finite signification prevail when

The applied science of theft suggests a heightened awareness of the flow
of events.
Appears to suspend
Buddha as interval
Not to end
Boxed in
Chronesthesia or the mental ability to travel in time, to relive past experiences
and imagine future experiences, does not exist.
Only tricks played by time
Present location unclear
Signs of impending rain
Exist
Rain itself
Exists

CRIME OR EVENT

Low risk high reward conventional arrangement
Series of undisciplined attempts within which it is possible to discern a
pattern of inaccurate but culpable decision making.
Behavior exacerbates excess
The same thing done by the same people in similar circumstances
When the trick of reality is played it follows that what is wanted is belief.
Inexorable fate and unbelievable luck are the same.
And occur at the same rate at the same time
Invisible activity or magical thinking the only possible reaction
To bring upon oneself, incur, to invite, to spite
Choice otherwise known as abomination is what concerns us here.
To take life
Buddha as event or
Things about which we have no information
Otherwise known as the perfect crime
Whether what has taken place is
Misplacement, positional panic or
Conceptual anarchy
The need to know (strong anxiety)
Someone is lying among the assumptions being given
Figure of the real or simplified equivalent
The choice is torn

IDENTITY

Someone is lying when the muscles around his mouth
Are the same as himself or itself
Known associates constitute a resource as well as a threat.
A person of the heart will find herself undefended or absent
Self-defendant, judge or scoundrel propose
A trivial distraction from the development of the profile
Network of differences and what appears to be body language with other cues
and then clues
Inferred by her story cause a sinking feeling in her auditor
An effect of eye movement
Object or suspect and then a tingling
Memory but not one's own when global variables are the most obvious place
to store data
Mug shot or something gold
Each object produces intense quiet
Or something old [section follows in mirror writing]
Reveals that whenever cleanup is needed by those active in the situation
They are innocent of nothing, pirate
Means fact as chance or change for its own sake
Actions equal the matter as in [end mirrored text]
What is the matter?
No right to the solution if obtained in this manner
No objection to the silence
Trend detection as mania, folksonomy or reverse allegory
Variations and departures from form as with bite marks, fingerprints,
skin, scum
Scram as in on the run
Implicates the unknown subject
Watching what continues to decay [no break here] or other image of being
Unmasked as if to say
Whose freedom?
It is you I accuse

DOCUMENT

No two people write alike
Bite marks are legible
Quills of another stripe also add up
Knowing this by knowing that
Situational syntax read as
The world of the crime or the whole world
Appears tangible, coherent, consequent
Not true or false until
Known even for a moment
As written chance
Does not exist as a person
Can be read or torn but
Can't be known
Greed, honesty, innocence, vanity
Eaten through
All right all night
Written down
Touched and gone

Speech

Text
Who that divines
Is destined
To say to see
Reality a ruse inasmuch as you can tag the real world
Invocation as about to be played again
Co-conspired to commune or commit
With apparent motive garbled and spoken softly, syntax and grammar
Or destination
A false negative when he said
We appear to be dealing with the embedded rhetoric of refusal
Shared guilt the individual bereft or unaware of
Payday play day or
Fallback position
Difficulty of reading
The current situation
Risk is not the only element of danger to be hidden
Measured or made
Mandatory in the worst case, anomalous gaping section left open
Alliteration as when
Something is suspended or hung
Caught in a lie, framed, contextualized
Heavenly justice or hired gun
Photographic evidence corollary to
Figure of the real represents defeat except when stated clearly
The subject is alive or is life
Being close to a personal limit of tragic proportions the individual before us
exists without doubt where to see is to be read or to be real or to be seen
Whatever happens unconcealed pleasure reveals
Nowhere to hide
No reason

In the Game

A move is a position
Including time and space
A play is an assertion or a decision
To play is to ply or capture
Or to form words out of given letters
Or to find items or destinations from which to launch in order to keep playing
Or to define a team or dream
Board games appear and must be played to the end
They differ in complexity and skill required
It is impossible to play to a draw
The only way to prevent your opponent from winning is to win yourself
In some rounds pieces can be promoted
Or cards dealt
Other plays require the writing of prosodized verbal units in prescribed forms
The rules are one's own
Or the drop rule applies
That a captured piece may be returned to the board as your piece or person
Identity may be further challenged
If you can complete one of three different structures from unbroken lines or paths
A ring, a loop or a fork
In any media at any time
Challenging all machine intelligence
Drawn as in hopscotch
Sung as in olly olly in come free
Named as when
Teams become interchangeable
Always a trick in which
The game can be yours
Or you can be the game

Who That Speaks

Spiritual things to spiritual people
War to warriors
Commons to communists
Decides to know nothing among you
When the impending crisis appears and
The present form of the world passes away
You speak into the air
The nothing that
Serves the creature rather than the Creator
Though not having the law, is a law unto himself
Itself (ourselves)
Lower limit even
Lower case
All of creation
Takes part
In the same nothing
When someone says
Seize the day
We speak in a human way

AGE OF PROPHECY

Prophecy of age
Edge of wings at the window
Late spring early evening
I remember the first war
The way the sky burned
Faces of angels destroyed
Cracking the glass
Not stopping
Part of God's plan or just the op
Roiling sky day for night
Night for night
Perched like a crow
Mortal for a moment
Things that fly fly
Children in Latin sing
Kiss of life kiss of death
Night out of sequence
No longer has the oracular organ
But rank and day job
A set of teeth like dice
His face the shape
Of a clever child or other animal
Says I'm tired but never sleeps
Dark soul can't rest or won't
You can't say soul
Where the dead angels are
Dressed in black and white
Whose names are sayings
That mean doubt or
The biggest secret ever
If you were a soul where would you go?
They used to hide
Tired of the war sick of dying
March with me etc
Sick of trying
Finds the medal in the ashes
Remnants in the steamer trunk
Whose past augers ill

Everyone has a side and
Knows too much or too little
Stucco walls wrought iron
The world ends in color
You're not from here they say
When I dream you again
The mine shaft blows
Ordinary sky
Clothes hung on lines
The air stream
The contrails
Breathing you in
Breathing you out
Can you tell me what you want?
Being easy to find is not
The only thing we have in common
Our script or battle plan or
War game whose combatants
Let the air out of each other
Strike after surgical strike
On this plateau
What's left of the plot
The ceremony is over
Or performance for which
Anyone might have taken the money
In the usual getup
Nails blackened cloth coat
Feathers leathers
The familiar road
Everyone on the side they're always on
The devil you know
I had a voice once
Removed from your sight
I saw for miles
Both of us alive then
All night talking
Hell loosed around

Enemies of bones
Shards of light
The horizon closing in
Someone says the ghost is gone
They drag you out by the heart
Coat open to the night
Prophetic arc
Unarguable result
Death after death
Splits into flight

Departures I-II /*War in Heaven*

1.

The line is monumental. Where does it end? My body can't remember we are here. Unaware of that. War hero. War chest. When did they start the war? The air is sucked out of it. I hear the sound in my head.

2.

Driving through fiction. It takes a long time to get to the airport. Airports are all the same. The wetlands of Hegenberger Road. Your Black Muslim Bakery. Oakland. No reserve seating. Tea. Dawn. Closed now. Rain in California.

"Or in the emptier waste, resembling air." Milton, *Paradise Lost*, 2:1045

A study of airports reveals they are the same only in feeling. Time zones specific to. Maintaining losses. Each of us banking over the coast. Cruising speed and altitude question the necessity to write out of a coherent self. The field explodes backward on the tape. "I was hung up on traveling." Atoms scatter during the feedback. Shortening the line. All the way down. Taking off he forgets his sweater. Acknowledges only the inner weather. And then not even.

3.

A letter not addressed to me and yet regarding my interests arrives in the morning. Readable poison. Addressed to my breath. Translucently curtained single window strategy. For the wind. For the air. Leaving the scavengers there. Southern California sound. Many stations away. Many bases. Threat assessment. This all happens in a 24-hour period. Six thousand years ago. "Who has displayed their glory throughout the heavens." The battle for the beginning. The Gideon bible is gold and somewhat dirty like the sun in the haze this morning. "The backward sun in philosophy." Alan Halsey

Continued haze the buildings are white. The palms endless. The park aquatic. They call themselves Ice Dogs, referring only to the white. Art Deco decays around us. The blondes in pastel. The blondes in black.

Weather girl. White Silk. A lactose-free organic soy milk has brought us this face. This speech.

"God I wish I'd never been traveling," Blaise Cendrars

4.

Highly uncertain at this point a primitive understanding obtains. Significantly, we have little predictive capability. Rush hour threat. No matter what point on the continuum we choose to measure, the measure remains the point. We are in the New Materials Age. We are cocked and ready to go.

Blurred distinction between war & peace. War & crime intertwine.

"Stripped of technical language," the thought stays in the air like a blast, like a crash, like a delirious cloud. Meaning is shredded around us like shrapnel, which also falls.

"Food gift from the people of the United States"

The Vincent Thomas Bridge in San Pedro. "US bombs too many to count today."

We go wheels up. All fifty states. "The tragedy of Andalusia." Andalusia the imagined state in a man's mind. He reclines odalisque on the tape. He is a traveler.

5.

The Portable Library

Books in heaven but not any book. Only as many as can be carried. As much as is allowed to be known. It takes five weeks for the information to cook in the system. After that whatever will happen has happened. The information, as always, is physical. "I would lose my mind if it weren't attached to my head." Multiplying along with thoughts of itself. A new terrifying coherency. Thoughtless grown.

Portable movies airport to airport. The future movies will be different each time they are viewed like a poem. The future is a disease. But only if you have it.

6.

I am here or rather there in that future danger. The realization now of clarity and presence. As an independent expert I monitor my breath, looking for evidence of change. I always find it. The illness is cultured and weaponized as a kind of memorial. The still-contaminated grave. The zinc-lined coffin. And finally there is never not the danger of breathing out. Breathing out in hazy calm. Olson believed in inertia, in going out by staying in. But in Southern California there is no difference. We want to be somewhere else. On another plane. Cold instead of warm. Transfer in Boston, Atlanta and Chicago. Phoenix. Vast carpet pattern. Air to air. Bombs. Missiles. Missives. Communicate the hard way.

"No reason for alarm. Keep monitoring the storm." There is no change. Or change threatens an imagined identity with an unimaginable clarity. The issues are basic, a matter of pride. Losing is unthinkable. The struggle is stalemated. There is no winning in real time or in real terms. The fight is symbolic. The plane is sacred. There is no agreement about what has happened or about what constitutes success or failure. The next thought is a sacrifice. The next act is a chapter. The radio is audible. Copy that.

"It is possible chemically to kill a person by inversion," Charles Olson. My body can't remember I am here. That factory is listed on no map. The remote site is only a whisper.

7.

Physics Today: Scattering allows a second line or combination of information to be received … with two independent signals communicated simultaneously the information transfer rate is increased. Two narratives recombine.

The Information War, as this is called, is where we live when we are home. We want more than one thing to know. We wanted it yesterday. Information was opposition. *Is opposition.* You said it.

"Even if we were able to solve these equations for a particular environment, the solution would change completely as soon as the environment changed. In reality, environments change all the time. Certain quantities vary from one disordered sample to the next. The properties of an ensemble of samples are studied. There is a decoherence rate. There are correlations."

8.

Absalom's Monument / Field Theory

Arch after arch of the recent future moves in unison. The wind like a train. The scale large. Faces illustrated and visible in planes. Pilots follow *Follow Me* trucks into empty space. Signs. Are these the End Times? A constantly addressed question. Hopeless. Open on the table.

"Nothing in her house. Nothing at work. Nothing in her mail. Nothing anywhere. Nothing we know."

Finally just another tourist destination. Airport transport transfer to another line. We don't have that kind of time anymore. It isn't mysterious. The voices are from the dead. The thoughts are also from there. All of them. We go on. The invasion of the dead takes place on the road. They squawk and cry. Never leaving us alone.

"We prefer micromechanisms to masternarratives."

An unstable assumption about the stable identity of the composer is a hidden but operative element in the story. In retrospect he is seen trapped in his car. Dying and falling. The theory comes out of him like sweat. The rules of engagement also break down. The resulting sound is final. Finite. It is a precise map of the event. The map is an argument. A plot against everything.

Each sequence is the breath of the dead. There is a depth to the grid. An underworld like the one at the airport. Things routed and broken open are kept moving nevertheless. This process is something other than it was. More intrusive and finally more destructive. It wouldn't have helped to know.

We obviously can't know. We are changed pronominally. We into them and I. Especially "I" though "I" am not what I was. What am I now? Absolute future. Getting out more or less alive. And what do "I" get? Do I get "you?" For a moment all of the physical assets are on the line. In the line.

Time goes by. The line ends. It is that time again. "time / is quantity where field is / millennia" (Olson). It is personal. More traditional than the old modernists and not recognizable as actors in the received sense, the new players take advantage of their invisibility to achieve unfamiliar new goals. It is a genre question. Is this winning or is this another monument that can never be finished? A tomb without a tenant. The tomb of the unknown soldier but not in the same way.

9.

Cosmic War / My Name is Sky

It's true but it doesn't help. They will attack in the next two days. We attack them. They us. They flee east and southeast and west and north. Now in prospect of the city. The sky burning or is it only the sun? We are already gone.

"Look long at this illuminated heaven—" "It is wrong to regard it other than critically." Lines from "The Murder of Khosrow" (Bihzad from the *Khamseh* of Nizami, 1494)

Flat maps of the sky. The light rolls across the table. Airport café rectangular window frames our activity. A home is destroyed. It stops us from thinking. Or sleeping. We wake up into sleep. Tired and hungry for sky.

Our picture of heaven is like a tower. We love our enemies. We listen for the light. The cursive version mimics the cloud. "My name is Sky," she says incidentally. The sky still sounds like an engine even after we have come down out of it. I had to admit I was asleep at the time. Yellow November. George Bush to John Wayne and onto the coast.

"The enemy is socially assembled." (*Terror in the Mind of God*) Everyone is a potential soldier. "We need sacrifices." We are an angry loner. Understandable and inevitable. Or a tree pushes out of the frame like a flame. The strategy is entirely symbolic. The space between us heats up. "Your last words," he says, "I already heard them."

"No one can predict the recombinant future." A stepped box encloses us. There is a monument in the interior. Access to the special lounge is guarded by soldiers. Indifference and satisfaction are made equal in a speech. Our distress is the subject. Things are twisted today. What is allowed to be in the sky?

An announcement comes over us. Embodied statement. Our faces hover under its halo. A hotel room in a ship in the air. We are in the air. The speech between us is what we breathe. There is static and presentation. There is a stage. This is a war. Miniaturized but cosmic in scale. This monumentality is not static in its display. Lives are not stable. Deaths are not counted. The deaths congregate and die. They die again. They fall down. Post field theory apocalypse. Only the page is left alive.

10.

A departure fails. A man with knives and a gun. X-ray vigilance. The explanation. "At the first sign of trouble, shoot them down." The nuns give their brains to science. How have you turned your experiences into books?

I don't know why they call it camouflage. We take off. We land again. Taking off is a rush. Landing is paradise. The airport is neutral. It has everything you need. Especially the nuts in orange cellophane and the zone reps boarding at your side. Everything but sleep which however some find there. Even here.

This kind of attack is not apparent when it happens, but only after years of propaganda. We are used to that. He wakes up and runs for his life.

"A morning in peacetime" (Chris Marker, *La Jetee*) "now seems far away. The man chosen to remember remembers nothing. Many died ... [when thought was stopped by time] ... Some thought they had won."

Always leaving/left with meaning. Given this knowledge. Given this situation I am also giving. (Going.) A man goes off on a plane. Announcing himself. Being announced all over the place. "I can't tell you that," he says, but he has a lot to say. He is definite. He is impatient with disagreement. "We are in this together," he says. "You are in this with me," he claims. But we are so over.

II.

In heaven there is no inner space, but at the airport there is plenty of territory overhead. Under the dome of the concourse there are chairs everywhere. In the great airports there is abstract expressionism on a heroic scale. There are armies and skeletons of beasts. Federalized pockets of concentration and transparent flow. With fear walking there is anxious rest and something like sky. Here there is time to look out, stopping to breathe and beyond that a windy corridor. The line moves in and out. This is a house with many doors. Floors like layers of heaven. Balconies. Mezzanines. Floodlit. Escalators. Stairways. Stairways to.

A figure twists and is constructed of minor materials. What is this device? What is it doing here? What is the mechanism? It allows for something like the tawdry religious engagement one might remember to feel just before boarding. Tactics are mixed in the field. The new precision has to do with use of vernacular form as opposed to mere speech which varies from place to place. Who will be next? you read on the sign about the lottery. Do you have to play to lose?

From time to time. These vernacular forms swarm around the local like cluster bombs. Many fronts open up. Many lines later. Radio contact is made. We are next. A satellite phone establishes our presence in the jeweled but pixelated spectrum of images streaming from there. Overwhelming force. You feel it in your chest.

An Air Force

I am born in the Air Force.

Preexisting condition

Eternall War

1 body

Will the force of the air create global cataclysm and despair?

In 1946 Tom Moriarty enlists in the Army Air Force at Fort Snelling in Minneapolis. He is 17.

Jack rabbits on the runway in waves

Where the periwinkle sky gives onto

Pictures of a childlike father in uniform.

I wait for something to happen that makes sense. Our neighbor is killed in Vietnam. He leaves a son behind who is my age. I am 12. It is 1964.

Excessive casualties with no strategic payback now as before

Orders

Ordinance

Stoicism

We move to Otis Air Force Base from St. Paul when I am 3. My parents have never heard of Cape Cod. They look it up in an atlas. Mae is a secretary for 3M, then called Minnesota Mining. She quits when she has me. Tom is a sergeant and jet mechanic. At Otis he will be on the C-121 Constellation, flying for the 961st Squadron of the Air Defense Command. His job as flight engineer is to keep the plane in the air. The version he flies, customized with a radar dome on top and an undercarriage full of surveillance equipment, is called a pregnant Connie.

Reconnaissance

Permanent change of station

Creative destruction

Cold war

Promotional opportunity

In Massachusetts there are hurricanes and snowstorms. Along with the rest of the guys in the flight crews, my father takes the planes to Bermuda whenever these occur, leaving us to dig out. This annoys my mother but we are self-reliant.

Bellicose intercepts

Eyes in the sky

57 bodies

While the fighting rages on

Tom could make more money by going to work for the airlines but he doesn't. The Air Force is a nonprofit organization with a mission. They have *esprit de corps*. Wearing his uniform, my father is well received wherever he goes. We all are. We are in the Air Force.

The blue from the skies

Intelligence is sent to the capital but is ignored.

An anamorph is a projection which distorts what we perceive.

"We will succeed unless we quit."

The mind becomes prey to delusions.

"He thinks he owns the world."

They ride out to Mormon Mesa to watch the mushroom cloud.

How much can you know? If you hear them fear them, they say, if you see them flee them, but it is always too late.

Leaflets say to leave but there is nowhere to go.

"I felt that people had no value," he said, "but became like animals, like simple fish."

Turning toward the war.

"They do their jobs," he said of the fighters, "and then they're home watching television."

They watch the war.

5 bodies

"Resistance is the only option. No one deserves this option."

Flesh and ichor

Beleaguered city

Unfiltered content

We arrive in 64, blasting along in an old Lincoln. My sister and I sleep in the customized back seat while Mae and Tom drive through the corn. We get to California in October. It is treeless and brown. I think I have never seen an uglier place. My parents are twenty years younger than I am now. Just kids.

Deployment

The bomb outside of town

Mantle of destiny

4 bodies

We live the news.

Mt. Rushmore and Rushmore Caves along the way. The Black Hills. My cream colored wool jacket and little scarf. The presidents loom in stone. My father looks forward to flying the new jet transport, the massive C-141 Starlifter. I look forward to it too.

"[W]ings of war"

Base library

Jihad Construction teaches organic farming and beekeeping.

The makeshift bomb shelter in the basement of our quarters on the Cape has a metal cabinet with water and soup in it. Canned fruit. We borrow stuff from it for daily life. My father's workshop is also in the basement. He fixes things.

I wake up thinking I don't remember my life, but don't I?

Plymouth Rock. Lilacs and sassafras. Woods Hole and Megansett Beach. Visiting the house of the scientist and his wife, I experience class for the first time. The wife does crafts with shells. She looks worried. They have a window seat. I want one.

Rockets are made of war.

Preemption

Stealth

We are the world.

"Mr. Devil"

Blows himself up.

It is possible for a rocket to strike you today. Right now!

Mae does ceramics, sews and paints. She makes poodle skirts for my sister and I. Tom prides himself on never having to take the car to the shop. He plays the piano. Standing in front of a mirror, he teaches himself the accordion.

Confidence in the government or lack thereof

"Disastrous rise of misplaced power"

Dwight D. Eisenhower.

Captain Kangaroo

Milk toast

Marilyn Monroe kills herself (so they say) in August 1962, the year before John Kennedy is killed. I would have been thunderstruck to know they were lovers.

Movies are a quarter at the base theater. On Sunday they are 50 cents. When I am 10 I chose to go to the movies instead of to church. I take 50 pennies out of the poker kitty and leave a note.

The Horse Soldiers

No death in heaven

Why We Fight

I don't know the prince of the powers of the air but I go to school with his kids.

My mother calls me in from playing outside so we can watch science fiction movies together. They scare the hell out of me but I like them.

"I don't work for the world, I work for the Air Force."

The Thing

When I run out of books to read in the base library my mother takes me to the tiny North Falmouth Library to get new Nancy Drews, Sherlock Holmeses and Jules Vernes. I walk into a jewelry store in Falmouth and ask to see the moonstones. They are brought out for me on a velvet tray. It is 1963. I am 11.

When cataclysm occurs you are in the center of the universe.

Is that how you feel?

"I want to get out of here," she says.

If there is a nuclear war I plan to go to Canada or Alaska but I know that really there is no place to go. I still know it.

Covenant Transport

"No element of judgment or prudential weighing of costs and benefits is acceptable in deciding whether or not to target civilians or take them hostage; it is always wrong."

Covenant Transport asks itself the question "Where does the path go from here?"

Life not insulated from what others do in your name.

Orange checkered water towers represent security to my mother and me when we see them from the road as we approach another base.

At Travis we go to the terminal to have their famous chili or to have hamburgers any time of the night or day. It is the main embarkation point for the war.

Unchecked exceptionalism

The walking wounded

Off we go

Robust rules of engagement. Lying low. Point of no return. My best friend and I climb over the fence surrounding the base pool in order to swim naked in it. We are 15. It is 1967. The Summer of Love.

"If the Americans leave, it will go back to killing in the streets," he said. "It will be civil war."

Base Exchange

The Doors

"They hold for honorable that which pleaseth/and for just that which profiteth"

Thucydides

I can't get no

Mounting tide of hopelessness

RAF Nimrod spy plane

We seek by lethal physical force to block and shatter their undertakings.

God's own mourning

Mother Travis appears at the ceremony expressing her complete support of the boys.

Originally, Travis Air Force Base is called Fairfield-Suisun Air Force Base. Suisun means west wind in Wintu. It is always windy there. In 1957 Brigadier General Robert F. Travis crashes his B-52 into a field where later an elementary school is built. The name is changed. My sister goes to the school. There is an atomic bomb on the plane.

Pageantry and sorrow

Soldiers and airmen

Women and children

41 bodies

"The map of my life is a circle," she begins. "I was born in the Air Force," she goes on. She wants to be able to get home in a hurry so she limits herself to a twelve block area.

The flight line

Cement Hill

Suisun Slough

Death toll

The problem with the kill-or-capture metric is that it has often been to the exclusion of having a deeper, richer understanding of the movement, its origins and our adversaries' mindset.

Resistance, rebellion and repression

My father's favorite actor is Burt Lancaster. He identifies with Lancaster's hatred of officers in *From Here to Eternity*. I identify with it too.

"This is the end, my only friend"

Incremental changes

"The aircraft lands at last without folding its wings"

It doesn't go off.

Me in a brown corduroy mini dress, listening to a cassette from my father in Vietnam. It is 1968. I am frowning.

A fractal set of hierarchies in the empire

Disaster possible and recurrent

The stalagmites of Rushmore Caves. Are we safe down there? Are we ever safe?

The base is a factory town with peace as its product, or war, depending on your point of view. Peace is our profession.

Curve tightens

Propagating a single narrative

I will not desert you.

If I am a boy my name is to be Daniel. Same with my sister. My aunt wants to name me Penelope. My father names me for the song. My mother wants to name my sister "Mariah" after another song. My father says he's not naming any kid of his after some damn storm. He says Diana Jean just rolls off the tongue. Finally my brother is born and is named Daniel. I am 13. I take Antoinette as my confirmation name when I become a soldier of Christ. I am the tallest person in my class. It is 1965.

My favorite poets are A.E. Housman and Vachel Lindsay.

"Abraham Lincoln Walks at Midnight"

Are brands more powerful than governments?

My brothers in arms

Another war brings up past wars. There are revolts and open displays of sorrow.

But such peace is partial, unstable and unsatisfying.

There could be concord and community and a shared sense of purpose and coordination—the flourishing of persons and communities.

Dream On

Early warning

"God doesn't live here," an American writes on an Iraqi wall. "This war is lost," he says. "No one understands what our mission is here. We aren't helping these people. We are just dying and getting injured. We fight for each other. We don't fight for the war."

65 bodies

The lottery

Outsourcing the conflict

Office of special plans

I grieved to that song.

My father flies troops to Vietnam and wounded men or bodies back. Sometimes he flies Vietnamese civilians around Vietnam, rescuing them from trouble. The C-141 can take off on a short runway. There are bullets holes in the fuselage. Combat pay.

Unintended consequences of secret operations

"They say that all good things must end some day."

Chad and Jeremy 1964

"Autumn leaves must fall."

Blowback

Driving cross country, I think of my next door neighbor and crush, Gary Bond. He is going with two girls, me and my best friend, Vonnie Sharkey. At night I can hear her father beat her mother. We are 12.

"I've dropped bombs before," he says.

Honor roll

Buzzards Bay

Martin Luther King is killed in April of 1968. Bobby Kennedy is killed in June. My father goes to Vietnam in August. We cry when he leaves. My mother leans for a last moment into the car that takes him away. We go inside. We wait for him to come back alive. I help my mother.

"We are the greatest force for good in the world."

John McCain

Human dignity

The junior class goes to see *2001: A Space Odyssey* at the Orpheum Theater in San Francisco. It is 1968. I am 16.

Three of my girlfriends join the service.

But I am not a soldier.

Cruel diabolical enemy finds great power by improvising

A blunt instrument aimed at civilians

"Wish you didn't have to go."

Steppenwolf

Big Brother

Cream

"No, no, no, no"

I read *The Rise and Fall of the Third Reich.* I identify with the victims. I
can't stop thinking about the war. I stop watching TV. My father comes
back. He wants to talk about the war but I can't bear to hear his stories. No
counseling is available for him or for me. I watch the moon on TV, staying
up all night with Walter Cronkite. I get pneumonia though it is summer. We
live off base but we are still in the Air Force. It is 1969.

Immense swept back wings of the B-52

Fifty miles away Robert Duncan is recovering from a biopsy for lung cancer.
He writes about it in a letter to Denise Levertov. He doesn't have it. "How
our few song birds here in the midst of the city rescue the morning." He is
50. 10 years older than my father.

"I feel free"

Falling prey to the tyranny of the majority or the will to get, expand and
retain power possessed by certain men.

The Jimmy Doolittle Museum

It is 1979 before I watch a war movie.

"…you've got to kill people, and when you've killed enough they stop
fighting"

Fresh outbreak of violence

"There was once a man…"

"He's out there without any decent restraint totally beyond the pale of any
acceptable human conduct."

"My only friend"

A woman on the radio thinks that air strikes are necessary to stop the genocide in Darfur. I think so too.

Another field trip

Gone With the Wind

Roadside bomb

Coordinated attacks

Rabbits disappear into the visible heat at the end of the runway.

My life as Jane Eyre

My life as Heathcliff

A people living in fear are not free.

A Flying Fortress can protect itself.

Tom is stationed in Pleiku in the Central Highlands. He studies Vietnamese. He makes friends with the Vietnamese firemen in the trailer by his. He is in charge of Transit Alert. He gives stuff to the Mountainard villagers who cluster by the base for safety. His friend, another sergeant, mixes Agent Orange. He tells us that we are bombing Cambodia though Nixon says we are not. I wonder how I can know something is happening when the news doesn't seem to know. I still wonder that.

Sabotaging the mechanics of power

"I know this goddamned life too well."

I read a biography of Nixon. It says that he can cry on cue.

My father makes friends with a band from the Philippines. He sits in with them on keyboards. I see a picture of my father with one of the girls in the band but then it disappears.

Stand By Me

"In the War now I make"

Revolt of the generals

Today's military.com

The class chooses "Bridge Over Troubled Water" as our graduation song.

It is 1970. Five more years of war.

Booby-trapped

Cut in half

Buried

Discovered beneath the truck

I give my virginity to my art history teacher at Sac State. Or perhaps he takes it. It is 1972. Nixon, Kissinger and Le Duc Tho negotiate in Paris.

You can still be drafted and die.

It is Halloween. After a demonstration, I ask my father to come and pick me up and he appears in his uniform. He looks very handsome. He is 10 years younger than I am now.

My boyfriend has a low draft lottery number. He pretends to be a heroin addict to get out of the war.

My Lai

The precise number killed varies from source to source, with 347 and 504 being the most commonly cited figures. There is a memorial on the site with 504 names.

Kent State

4 dead, 9 wounded when the National Guard opens fire on a demonstration by students.

Christmas bombing

All in the Family

Bring the war home

Anything you can know about it is more than you can know.

"They're worse than the brownshirts and the communist element and also the nightriders and the vigilantes," the governor of Ohio says. "They're the worst type of people that we harbor in America. I think that we're up against the strongest, best-trained, militant, revolutionary group that has ever assembled in America."

Fiasco

State of Denial

"Into my heart an air that kills"

The Air Force Memorial opens in Washington D.C. Its three huge spires mimic a maneuver performed by the Blue Angels and the Thunderbirds called the bomb burst.

They force your eyes up into the air.

Absent without leave

Awarded posthumously

"It is portentous, and a thing of state"

The war ends. My I.D. card expires. I am no longer in the Air Force. I am 23. It is 1975.

Loon Woman

Eternall War

Tomb of the Unknowns

My father has an aneurysm and ends up in the VA Hospital in Minneapolis where *Born in the U.S.A.* was made. He has skin problems from exposure to Agent Orange but he doesn't die of it. My mother goes to visit him every day. He dies of something else.

Scores of bodies

Failed state

Chain of command

My parents are buried next to each other in the Fort Snelling National Cemetery in Minneapolis. Endless white stones.

The glory

BLOOD SUBJECT

Two Modes

Two modes of representation are tearing time apart.
        Luce Irigaray, *Speculum of the Other Woman*, translated by Gillian C. Gill

Not sexually neutral
The uncontainable volume comprises
Specific visionary actions
The exposure of theory by practice
Ariadne abandoned on Naxos
Flesh made word or
A disruptive excess overwhelms
The founding obliteration
Again against and
Outside of discourse but on the earth
Where objects are possibilities
Flesh made word
But A is not B
A is just not fucking B
The unconscious has a history
A symbolic redistribution
The sensible split off from the intelligible
Violent hierarchy
Wakes on the beach
Assumes the utopian position
A speech act that
Desires others
To speak and act
Is that too much to ask?

Snow Red Rose White

Opens with the snow

Or of a glass with its sex intact

High on her mountain

To be female is to be

Matter, the mere absence of Reality

Contempt for form as such

Who does not participate in ideas

atypical, atopical not only not good but evil

no gaze, no "natural light"

without which to repeat nothing exists

no common sense, easily distracted

Nothing has a price in this divine consummation

This "flowing, restless reality"

Doesn't want what you're selling

Mysticism, mystery, hysteria, hystera

"thinking tissue," waste, refuse

"I think, therefore God is"

He says to her

That she has no limits

In her fallen state

Impenetrable much less than if penetrable

With hands clasped as snow

Also called white bees
Sees themselves, herself, itself

"Piece together the ice-puzzle of reason"

Renter/Rented

"imagine that woman imagines"
The limit of opacity
Each subject requires
To know itself as the same

When the "object" speaks
The inertia of dreams also muteness
Ceases to be while
Resemblance proliferates

Without reflection
In a space so negative that
She, Satanic,
Overthrows the plan where

Trapped in the same economy
Unowned self or name (she rents)
Who is not the same
Mirrors only the mirrored world

Not questioned or questioning
But consistent
With (again) mirrors, surfaces, screens, supports
Unsupported

Everything sleight
Forms illusions etc
Weaponized
Ontic because

Hidden in its rented crypt where no one (even) skilled philosophers has
glimpsed its "inability to recognize divinity within which leads to casting
reality out"

Intuition of a woman
Frozen when
"limits bind the heart"
Possessing only

Never Returning Time

Divine category, object or person
Not dead but lost
Or boxed limited to
Consuming or consumed by
Fruit from goblins or
A bug like a skull
Entity or animal
Wants things, people, satisfaction
Disappears into nature (is nature)
But the vegetables no longer prove anything
I must have eaten them
Am them, "it" if
Men then women
Divisive categories
Ladies and Death
So-called enchantment
Furze, heath, tufts, gorse, gorged
On thorns indiscreet indirection
Has not yet taken place
But is (again) *a* place or
Never returning time
"Woman is a common noun for which no identity can be defined."
"Her shining raiment, her gleaming skin conceal the disaster within"
The kiss (trick) which
breaks the spell until (she)
unredeemed, illusive and preoccupied
With enveloping discursivity
An agreeable object in the landscape of existence
Enclosed by glass wakes to
Reveal nothing reflecting back
In a contingent therefore empty room
Now I lay me down into
Freedom as the moment of this doom
The fortress of sleep

The Other/Woman

What is it? What am I?

I am regarded as the other woman by another woman inaccurately. Her husband has a cat and my stepdaughter is allergic to cats, so I can't (this is a dream) have been in any sense, the other woman. The police have the other woman surrounded on another matter but she—we come to an understanding about this—will never give up.

"Foul or female"

fine or fire, but in fact, what is that?

She is said to perform her duties less well

Being body shaped by intention unbodied

...that still *center*, *undifferentiated* and circular, whose admitted motive force seems to work on the *outer edge of its orbit*.

Censored out of present existence

Like a plant

Provides evidence only if

For woman read worker or other who

May just as well not be as be but is

Divinating (let's say)

In faith or fate

Not a metaphor not inevitable

The event is gender the deity female

The power not one of belief but of being

You or I who am

Divine

Blood Subject

Buries the dead
Takes upon herself destruction by fire
By placing in the womb of the earth
Preserves her kinsman from desire
Where rose trees bloom
Next day a clear frost
The glass mirror window whose
Ice against heat
Against hate
Frames the place
Where only brother and sister or sister and sister
Whose same blood and name
Apple problem and tragedy of being born
Are arranged together but she
Can't talk to the king hence
Walled up alone
Damned by consenting to a punishment
Not merited yet can't escape
Where birds and bears also mute
Can't bite back (like the apple) or can
Like the animal
So remains fake alive
Until stock jealousy of aging queen
(False mirror) kills self or someone else
Not knowing why until
Knock at the door must be a traveler
A bear is there (blood subject)
Or a body
And she recites
"Snow White Rose Red
Don't beat your lover dead"
Walled in where femininity dies
And nothing can excuse the crime or minimize the punishment
But where is the body?
How big is the bear?
Caught a piece of herself in the door
Thought she saw gold
Or was it fire

Mixed with her own hair
The unconscious while remaining unconscious
 is supposed to know the laws of consciousness
which is permitted to remain ignorant of it (her)
and will become more repressed as a result of failing to respect those laws
perpetuating an inner dilemma and outer story
where again she is walled up
Fear anger surprise disbelief but not enough
Rose Rose and Snow Red
Woman as guardian of the blood.
But as both she (woman) and it (the blood)
have had to use their substance
to nourish the conscious self,
it is in the form of bloodless shadows (unconscious fantasies)
that they maintain (barely)
an underground subsistence.
Snow White marries the prince; Rose Red the brother
Only the bear remains
And the body
Blood subject

ARIADNE'S LAMENT

Where languid fates
Ubiquitous
Like crows or women
Or men whose pledges
Not by definition
As real as their wars
Or their needs, leave

Nymphs meaning women
Already where
A god arrives late suggesting
Possession as a form of knowledge
Wears itself out
When nymphs appear
The divine material begins to throb
They are the medium where gods and
Adventurous men meet
But we are not men

If chaos is sacred to us
There is no relief
And if female
We are perceived
As not being
The ritual changes
What doesn't exist
Invented each time
The idea of the divine
Where stolen subjectivity is
Ransomed for all of life
And all of time
Where later as wife
But too late
The soldier
Set her mind alight

.Where one must not learn
But be in a certain state

God as mental event
Is not theirs (or ours) or was

Her destiny to generate
Emerge, linger, endure
Reverse engineer
Posit new values
Free, autonomous, sovereign
Setting, framing, mounting, glazing
"a woman alone goes from darkest
to most sublime of the divine."
Raped. Robbed. Robed.
(Weds the god)
"the finery needed to capture the idea"
Inside limitless outside old
Subtle, insidious, incomprehensible
Enslaved to an idea
May be read as: she gave herself
Out to be: what she was not
Amazed, enmeshed, incensed

Scheming, seductive, foreign,
Realigned, redacted, unsaved, reenacted
Women play out
Women—the series.
Woman—the game.
A blank left blank
Poses, proposes, offers what
Burdened by love
Unsupported or known
By heart

A priestess in a religion whose origins are false
In a stone house where wood burns
And there is a forest or some trees
A meadow drowned
And beyond that, water
All the water in the world

All the time
Frozen, melted, frozen again
Fragmented as with power lost
Useless premonition
Necessary, fruitful, imaginary
Morphological marks of her fluid,
Plural, nonlinear skin
Knowledge always passion
Not visible because inside
Sex meaning yours or mine

Ariadne bears a perfect resemblance
But to what?
Stunned by emotional death
They saw they said
She "set herself up"
Recognized late the traitorous gesture
Which was her own
And its echo
Languished to wait
For a good marriage but was it?
You said she said
(He speaks in her voice)
Why all this affliction?
You—executioner—god!
Or am I a dog
To wallow before you?
My companion
My splendid enemy
Always jealous
Always with reason
To whom I was
Never not unfaithful
But attached, attracted, exacted
Until finally gone
What did I see when I saw you
That spoke silently through
and beyond the words
Not you Not that

ORDINARY LOVE

Intact
Or horizon
Whose planes of the world
(A not B etc)
I am and see
A nonlimited spot
Of freedom with desire
Not the same or different
Not sequence or distance
Or in relation
Though related
As in recognition
I (you) of you (me)
Each another multiple
Going out into
Nonappropriated unreconstructed
Space beyond
What we are
That we know
Exiled in Any One
Self-affection
Silent though silence
Not unlike whatever
Isn't enough
Is ordinary
(The final premonition)
Is home

NOTES

Page 5

Luce Irigaray, *Sexes and Genealogies*, translated by Gillian C. Gill (New York: Columbia University Press, 1993, p. 6).

Page 49

"WELCOME DEAR CHAOS" is a line by Michael McClure from *Plum Stones* (O Books, Oakland, 2002, p. 63).

The 27 words by Bruce Conner used in the present poem were supplied by Bruce Conner to the author in 1975 in response to a request for words made when sending him the text of the poem "Waking From Sleep a Thousand Miles Thick," which used words from a sculpture by Conner and Michael McClure called "Cards & Tables." "Waking From Sleep a Thousand Miles Thick" is the first poem in *A Semblance: Selected and New Poems: 1974–2007* (Omnidawn).

Page 56

Alan Halsey claims not to have provided words for this poem.

Page 89

"Companion Studies," *Wittgenstein's Devil*, Alan Halsey (Stride Publications, London, 2000, p. 76).

Blaise Cendrars, *Selected Writings, Prose of the Trans-siberian & of the Little Jeanne de France*, translated by Tony Baker (West House Books, Sheffield, 2001).

Page 90

"A Bibliography in America," *Collected Prose of Charles Olson* edited by Donald Allen and Benjamin Friedlander (University of California Press, Berkeley, 1997).

Page 92

Bihzad: Master of Persian Painting, Ebadollah Bahari, (St. Martin's Press: New York, 1996).

Germs: Biological Weapons and America's Secret War, Judith Miller, Stephen Engleberg and William Broad (Simon & Schuster: New York, 2001).

Page 102

"No element of judgment or prudential weighing of costs and benefits is acceptable in deciding whether or not to target civilians or take them hostage; it is always wrong."

Harry S. Stout, *Upon the Alter of the Nation: A Moral History of the Civil War* (Viking: New York, 2006).

Page 104

"The aircraft lands at last without folding its wings" Guillaume Apollinaire, "Zone," *Alcools, Selected Writing of Guillaume Apollinaire*, translated by Roger Shattuck, 1971, p. 119).

Page 106

"God doesn't live here..." "Endurance Meets doubt In Iraq," Michael R. Gordon, *New York Times*, September 3, 2006.

Page 110

"In the War now I make" Robert Duncan, "Passages 27," *Bending of the Bow* (New Directions: New York, 1968, p. 120).

Page 115

Luce Irigaray, *Speculum of the Other Woman*, translated by Gillian C. Gill (Cornell: Cornell UP, 1985, p. 353).

Laura Moriarty was born in St. Paul, Minnesota, and grew up in Cape Cod, Massachusetts, and in Northern California. She attended the University of California at Berkeley. She has taught at Naropa University and Mills College and is now the Deputy Director of Small Press Distribution. Awards include Poetry Center Book Award in 1983, a Wallace Alexander Gerbode Foundation Award in Poetry in 1992, a New Langton Arts Award in Literature 1998 and a Fund for Poetry grant in 2007. Recent books include include *A Tonalist* (Nightboat Books, 2010), *A Semblance: Selected and New Poems, 1975–2007* (Omnidawn, 2007) and the novel *Ultravioleta* (Atelos, 2006).

NIGHTBOAT BOOKS

Nightboat Books, a nonprofit organization, seeks to develop
audiences for writers whose work resists convention and
transcends boundaries. We publish books rich with poignancy,
intelligence, and risk. Please visit www.nightboat.org to learn
about our titles and how you can support our future publications.

The following individuals have supported the publication of
this book. We thank them for their generosity and commitment
to the mission of Nightboat Books:

Elizabeth Motika
Benjamin Taylor

Nightboat Books gratefully acknowledges support from The
Fund for Poetry, the National Endowment for the Arts,
the New York State Council on the Arts Literature Program,
and the Topanga Fund, which is dedicated to promoting the
arts and literature of California.